DEBT NEGOTIATION

BY
Wilfred Coombs

First Printing, June 2013

Published by DebtPros21.

DebtPros21 is dedicated to educating consumers about the credit industry. For more information please visit our website at *www.debtpros21.com*, or write to us at:

DebtPros21
401 Cooper St.
Taylor, PA 18517

Author: Wilfred Coombs
Chief Editor: Kenn Anderson, Jr.
Layout and Design: Kenn Anderson, Jr.

ISBN13: 978-0-9895831-6-9

Foreword

During my many years in business, I have been both a debtor and a creditor at the same time. Playing both roles simultaneously has taught me much about the basics of negotiating. There were times when my business suffered cash shortfalls and I was forced to contact my creditors and ask for some forbearance in paying my debts in order to remain in good standing with them. At the same time, I had to be in touch with my customers and offer them incentives to pay their bills more promptly. Below are some of the things I have learned from that experience.

- Wilfred Coombs

DEBT NEGOTIATION

DEBT NEGOTIATION

BE PREPARED

Before you pick up the phone and call your creditors, make sure you know where you stand financially. Put together a comprehensive monthly income statement showing all of your income and all of your expenses and come to an accurate bottom line. It's important to do it month by month because both may fluctuate significantly during the year. Once your statement is complete, look at your obligations for each creditor and decide upon the most realistic payment arrangements you can afford for each (more on this later).

Dan Shapiro, an expert on successful negotiation practices, pre describes the value of creating a positive and more productive negotiating environment, and lays out 5 core emotional concerns that need to be met in order to accomplish this. This lesson is derived from Big Think Edge, an online learning platform designed to help employees help their companies cultivate the new skills and knowledge necessary to invent new products, new markets, new business models, and new industries.

Shapiro tells us that people have the tendency in negotiation to focus on the facts and the figures, ignoring the emotional component. Together with his colleague, Roger Fisher, Shapiro has boiled down a person's "complex sea of emotions" into a handful of things that he calls Core Concerns -- matters that are important to all of us. "Your ability to deal with these core concerns, five of them, will bring you power," Shapiro says.

1.) **Appreciation.** Do you feel appreciated by that other person in the negotiation? And. . . . Do you think they're feeling appreciated by you?
2.) **Autonomy.** Autonomy is the freedom to make decisions without somebody else imposing a decision on you. You walk in to that negotiation and you tell that other party, "Here's the proposal; take it or leave it." Guess what they're more likely to do? To leave it. It has nothing to do with the rationality of the negotiation; it has everything to do with the process with whether that other person's autonomy feels respected or imposed upon, impinged upon.
3.) **Affiliation.** Rather than taking the adversarial positional approach, consider what the emotional connection is like between you and the other person or group?
4.) **Status.** Who feels respected for their status? Who feels disrespected? "As the only female in this room, what's your perspective?" Not cool. Respect people's status.
5.) **Role.** Do people have a meaningful role in the negotiation? "You have great power to actually structure the roles that you play and the others play in the negotiation to help you reach some sort of mutual gains," Shapiro says, "where you both are better off than you otherwise could be."

So before your next negotiation, Shapiro's recommendation is to walk through these five core concerns. It doesn't need to take more than five minutes. But here's the advantage you will gain. "Before your next negotiation you already know five things about that other person," says Shapiro. That means you will walk in much more prepared, and ultimately a more powerful negotiator.

BE HONEST

Never try to deceive or lie to your creditors. Tell them exactly what your situation is and what you feel is the best arrangement you can make with them for paying your obligations. Have evidence in the form of an income statement ready to go, if necessary, that will reinforce what you tell them verbally.

GET IN FRONT OF YOUR PROBLEMS

Recently, many people suffered great financial loss as a result of hurricane Sandy. If I was advising them financially, I would tell them to contact all of their creditors, secured and unsecured, and ask them for temporary payment arrangements that would allow them to remain in good standing until things get back to normal. There are a number or different approaches they can take depending on their situation, some examples are:

6.) Lower monthly payments – Once you have completed your monthly statement and have an accurate picture of you finances, you should be able to determine how much of your monthly payment you can afford for each creditor.

7.) Prioritizing - If you determine that you cannot afford to pay every creditor every month immediately, you must prioritize your list of creditors according to their level of importance.

8.) Forbearance - For those creditors you cannot pay immediately, you must contact them and ask for forbearance. It means you are asking them to suspend your payments for a few months and then adding those payments on to the end of the loan or resuming them at a higher level once you are back to normal.

I realize this can be a daunting task for many people. It is embarrassing to contact your creditors and tell them you have difficulty paying your bills. You feel like you are admitting that you cannot properly manage your finances. While you are in the process of convincing yourself this is the right thing to do, remember this.

1.) You are not alone. Since the recession of 2008, thousands of people have been forced to default on their financial obligations. In fact, the major banks and credit card companies have created create new departments just to deal with delinquent accounts.
2.) Your creditors will appreciate your honesty and candor in dealing with your problems and they are equally as anxious to find a solution that is amenable to both of you. Further, it costs them money to try to collect on delinquent accounts. They would like to avoid those costs, if possible.
3.) If you can convince them that you are eager to make an honest arrangement that allows you to meet your obligations to the best of your ability; they will usually work with you.

IF YOU ARE ALREADY DELINQUENT

Accounts that are already delinquent require a similar approach as just described, but there are some significant differences. First, let's review the various methods companies use to manage delinquent accounts.

When a creditor refers an account to collections status, there are a variety of approaches they may take in their attempt to collect the money they are owed. Some examples are:

- **They can contract with a collection agency and offer them a commission if they collect the amount owed.**
- **They can sell the account to a collection agency, or to another lending agency, for an amount below that which is**

owed, leaving the new owner of the account to settle with the debtor.

- **In many cases, they will contract with more than one collection agency on a commission basis at the same time, hoping to increase their chances of collecting.**

Obviously, the approach they actually take will depend on the size of the debt obligation and whether it is secured or unsecured.

WHAT ARE YOUR OPTIONS?

Our "Manual for Consumers" publication lays out in some detail the legal basis you have for settling your debts and the procedure you should follow in that process. Before you decide on a specific process, however, you need to do some research.

1.) Who currently owns the account? By now, you might be getting a series of what they call "dunning" letters and phone calls from a collection agency. You should contact the original creditor and ask them if they still own the account. If they do, it means they are still in control of the settlement process and amount. Ask to speak to someone in charge of settling the account and try to negotiate a settlement with them directly. Obviously, what you are doing here is eliminating the middle man, which could save you both time and money.

    If the creditor refers you to a collection agency, it means they have either sold the account to that collection agency or they have a contract with them that guarantees the contractor a commission on the settlement.

2.) If the account has been sold – It means that the original creditor has already given up on collecting the debt and has written it off of their taxes as a loss. If the debt is more than six months old, banking regulations sometimes require that the debt be written off. In that case they have sold the account for pennies on the dollar and the collection agency does not need to collect anywhere near the full amount to make a profit. If this is the situation, it probably means that the account has been delinquent for more than a year and a lot of time and money has already been spent trying to collect from you.

This could work to your advantage. The collection agency is usually willing to settle in these cases for a fraction of the full amount. It means you can start the negotiation process by offering a low settlement amount, as little as twenty five cents on the dollar, and see what happens.

The procedure above applies mainly to "unsecured" debt, meaning debt that is not attached to any type of collateral. The process changes significantly if the debt is either a mortgage or a car loan. In these, your negotiation is about avoiding repossession or foreclosure.

WHAT IS FORBEARANCE?

Let's go back to the victims of hurricane Sandy. Hopefully, their situation is temporary, meaning that they will eventually recover both mentally and financially. Accordingly, they are asking their creditors for a payment arrangement they can live with until they get back to normal. The forbearance can either be an agreement to make lower payment for a period of time or postponing the current payments and adding them to the term of the loan.

Now you may not be the victim of a hurricane, but you might have recently experienced a temporary financial setback due to a variety of factors, which may include a lay off from you or your spouse's employment or an expensive medical procedure, but the same principal applies. Get out in front of the problem and contact you secured creditors.

DO NOT WAIT FOR A FORECLOSURE OR REPOSSESSION NOTICE

If you have already received such a notice, you should probably retain the services of an attorney. Once these processes go into effect, they are automatic and can be hard to reverse. If you have not yet received such a notice, contact your creditor immediately and begin negotiating with them before the situation falls out of control.

MAKING AN OFFER OF SETTLEMENT

Let's say you currently have a number of revolving (i.e. credit/charge cards) accounts that are delinquent. It probably means that your financial situation is not good and your income is not sufficient to pay off these delinquent accounts. Again, I reiterate, you must sit down and construct a careful accounting of your finances. Your income, expenses, delinquent debts, and any future obligations not yet due must be included. For more information on how to construct such a statement, please refer to our publication entitled "The Ten Commandments of Credit".

Once you have done this correctly, you should have enough information at your disposal to make two basic decisions:

1.) Prioritizing all or you debts in the proper order – Listing all of your debts in order of importance and developing a strategy for settling those that are the least important and keeping the most important ones in good standing.
2.) Determining the amount you can afford to offer to offer those that are delinquent so they can be settled.

Once you have completed the process, it is time to begin to settle the delinquent accounts. Below is the process you should utilize:

1.) Settle the smallest accounts first – We suggest the approach because the smallest debts are usually the easiest to settle and it will give you the necessary practice and confidence you need communicate effectively with creditors.
2.) Always follow up your offer in writing, whether the creditor accepts it or not. Written confirmation of you offer is very important. It acts as evidence that you are making a serious effort to settle the debt and can be used as evidence in court, if necessary.(more on this later).
3.) Send a copy of your written offer to the credit repositories. Once Equifax, Trans American and Experian know that you have made a settlement, they will usually follow up with the creditor and urge them to respond in writing.
4.) Make a file for each creditor and document all offers, both verbal and written – You may need all of this information if the creditor decides to sue you.
5.) Initiating collection procedures in order to collect a delinquent debt can cost your creditors money. They would prefer not to incur these costs and would rather reach a reasonable settlement with you.

WHAT ABOUT DELINQUENT TAXES??

Many people are under the mistaken assumption that these rules do not apply to delinquent taxes. Not true. Governments at all levels are willing to negotiate with you just as private companies are. You can use exactly the same process as we described above to negotiate with the IRS or State and Local tax agencies.

WHAT IF YOU ARE SUED??

If you receive a summons to appear in court because you have been sued by a creditor, here is our advice:

1.) Don't Panic!! – The creditor or collection agency is just trying to force a settlement so they can get paid.
2.) Always appear at the hearing!! If you don't show, the hearing officer will assume that you don't care about the outcome and will usually grant the creditor whatever settlement they ask for.
3.) Take your files with you – Again, preparation is the key to success. Have your income statement with you as well as any written settlement offers you have previously mad to the creditor.
4.) Make sure the judge or hearing officer understands that you have made a concerted effort to settle the account. Impress upon them that the offer you already made is the best you can do under your current circumstances.

MAKING YOUR PAYMENT

Hopefully, the settlement you negotiate is exactly what you asked for and you can take care of by making one payment. In many cases, however, the settlement amount is more than you can pay in one installment. You must assume that this will happen and think about an installment plan that you can afford. When you are negotiating this plan, follow these rules. Finally, be sure to use certified checks or money orders so you will have a proper receipt.

No interest or carrying charges – Let's say you agree to pay the settlement amount over three months. Before you begin, ask for a written agreement from the creditor that the payments will simply divide the settlement amount in three equal installments with no charges.

ASK FOR REMOVAL

The Fair Credit Reporting Act stipulates that a delinquent account can remain son your credit report for "up to" seven (7) years. Most people, including many of your creditors, are under the impression that it says a minimum of seven years. Not True!! Once an account is settled and the settlement is paid, the creditor can remove it any time. This is especially true if the creditor is a third party, such as a collection agency. They are not the original creditor once the account is settled, there is no reason for their information to remain on your report.

One of the reasons this does not occur as much as it should is the three credit repositories discourage creditors from removing the information before the seven year maximum. There are a variety of reason for this, and the repositories may try to discourage your creditor from taking this action, but if the creditor insists, they must remove it.

For this reason, you should follow up after the payment is made to make sure that the removal has been accomplished.

FILING BANKRUPTCY

You may be thinking of consulting and attorney about your situation. Not a bad idea, but remember that most attorneys will advise you to file bankruptcy. If you are seriously in debt and have few or no resources to pull you out it, bankruptcy is certainly a legitimate alternative. There are some disadvantages to filing bankruptcy, however, that you need to consider.

1.) Bankruptcy stays on your credit report for up to ten years. That means that any time during that period you try to borrow money from a secured lender, you will have to face considerable scrutiny about your financial history.
2.) The new bankruptcy laws passed by congress in 2003 make the process much more difficult and no longer excuses you from paying those old debts.
3.) For more information on the current bankruptcy laws, see page 11 of the basis of credit knowledge or review the following website: http://www.uscourts.gov/FederalCourts/Bankruptcy/BankruptcyBasics/Chapter7.aspx

TAX CONSEQUENCES

Depending on your financial condition, any savings you get from debt relief services can be considered income and taxable. Credit card companies and others may report settled debt to the IRS, which the IRS considers income, unless you are "insolvent." Insolvency is when your total debts are more than the fair market value of your total assets.

DEBT SERVICES

After reviewing the above information if you decide that you will let someone else deal with your creditors, that's up to you, but be careful!! There a number of disreputable organizations out there that will take your money and, in some cases, make your problems even worse. The Federal Trade Commission offers some sage advice on selecting a company or agency to assist you in this effort. A summary of that information is located at http://www.consumer.ftc.gov/articles/0150-coping-debt.

I HAVE DELINQUENT MEDICAL BILLS?

In my ten plus years of experience in helping consumers with their credit problems, I can't count the number of times I have watched people access their credit information and be immediately shocked at seeing delinquent medical bills in their credit reports. Their first response the revelation is usually something like, **"I thought my insurance company took care of these bills??"** Well, obviously they didn't. Why?

There could be a number of reasons, but it usually boils down to a bureaucrat inside of your insurance company that rejects your claim on some technicality. For example, if your plan is part of an HMO, it may be rejected because you did not obtain prior approval from them, even though your physician may have recommended that you have the test done at the particular lab or clinic.

These issues usually arise after you have had surgery. Before the operation your doctor usually orders a number of preliminary tests to make sure the surgery is necessary. Then you have the procedure and when you come home and are recuperating, the barrage of correspondence from the hospital and doctors' offices begins to come in the mail. "THIS IS NOT A BILL" or "YOU MAY BE PARTIALLY RESPONSIBLE FOR THESE CHARGES." At some point you become confused and you make the mistake of depending upon your medical insurance provider to sort things out for you. Unfortunately, that's a mistake. This is especially true if you are on Medicare and you have supplemental insurance to pay for the cost the government doesn't cover.

You can never assume that your supplemental insurance provider will pay the costs not covered by Medicare without verifying that it will happen. Many older people have made this assumption over the years it has resulted in them having credit problems for bills that are usually small in relation to the total cost of the surgery.

WHAT CAN I DO??

1.) Contact the medical facility where you had the test done and ask them why the bill was not paid. If they tell you that you insurance company denied the claim, contact you insurance agent and ask them to find out why the decision to deny the claim was made and whether it can be reversed. During the conversation, you should impress upon them that the procedure was ordered by your physician and proof that it was performed is on file.
2.) If you are unsuccessful, then look at your credit report and determine whether the medical facility is still in charge of the bill or if it has been referred to a collection agency.
3.) In either case, refer to the procedures below and settle the account. As I said previously, the majority of these delinquencies are small. They average around $150.00 so there will be little room for negotiation.
4.) Follow these steps:

a.) Contact the agent and as then to send you a letter stipulating the amount you have to pay to settle the account in full. The letter should also stipulate that, once the full amount is paid, they will contact the three credit repositories and notify them that the account has been settled.
b.) Once you have received the letter send them a certified check or money order so you will have a copy.
c.) Send a copy of your letter to the three credit repositories listed below. Why? Collection agencies are famous for not updating the information on credit reports. As a result, you may settle the account and find out a few months later that your credit report still shows the account as delinquent.

CREDIT BUREAU INFORMATION

Equifax
P.O. Box 740241
Atlanta, GA 30374-0241
(800) 685-1111

Experian
P.O. Box 2002
Allen, TX 75013
(888) EXPERIAN (888-397-3742)

Trans Union
P.O. Box 1000
Chester, PA 19022
(800) 916-8800

ABOUT THE AUTHOR

Wil Coombs has been an entrepreneur since 1982. In 1986 he founded the Education and Training Center, a company designed to provide low income individuals and single moms with the opportunity to learn competitive job skills. Once they were trained, he and his staff would assist them in finding full time employment. After a time, he realized that one of their biggest obstacles was their total lack of credit worthiness.

Years later, he developed a friendship with John Hudock. John was an expert on credit and credit scoring and published many articles on the subject, including a monthly piece in the Mortgage Press, a nationwide publication for mortgage brokers. In 2000 John formed a company called The International Credit Club. It was designed to help people with serious debt problems to restore them to financial health.

John and Wil worked to develop a guide for the consumer that would help them "bootstrap" themselves into financial solvency. During that process, they worked one on one with a number of individuals with serious financial issues. John's expertise combined with the experience they both gained from their experience resulted in numerous successes and The International Credit Club continued to grow.

Sadly, John passed away in 2008 and the company was dissolved, leaving Wil with a wealth of knowledge he could use to help people help themselves. Recently, he decided to utilize the Internet to disseminate that information to anyone who could use it to their benefit.

Wil Coombs founded DebtPros21 in order to distribute the information that he has collected during his many years of experience in the field of consumer credit counseling. His goal is to educate consumers so that they can make intelligent decisions about their debt problems and, hopefully, resolve them on their own.

For more information, please check out these other publications from DebtPros21.

Reading Your Credit Report

This book guides you through each individual trade line and tells you the significance of each piece of information as it applies to your credit worthiness, as well as the proper procedures for disputing errors on your credit information.

The Credit Industry - A Primer

Learn about how to read your credit report, protect yourself from predatory lenders and debt collectors, as well as how to safeguard yourself from credit fraud and identity theft.

The Ten Commandments of Credit

Intended to be used after your credit has been restored, *The Ten Commandments of Credit* will give you the information you need in order to maintain excellent credit worthiness.

ISBN 978-0-9895831-6-9
9 780989 583169